Annemrie Nikolaus
Aquitaine: The End of a War
By the Wayside...

Legal notice:
"Aquitaine: The End of a War. *By the Wayside...*"
Written By Annemarie Nikolaus
Originally published in German as: Aquitanien: "Das Ende eines Krieges. *Am Rande des Weges... *"
Copyright © 2014-2016 Annemarie Nikolaus, 03240 Tronget/Allier, Frankreich
Translated by Melody Shaw
Cover Design © 2016 Design Annemarie Nikolaus, Foto © 2010 Jean-Bernard Nadeau
All rights reserved
ISBN: 9782902412808

ANNEMARIE NIKOLAUS

By the Wayside ...

AQUITAINE: THE END OF A WAR

Contents

Introduction

Each year, in a town near the Dordogne River, not far from Bordeaux, a performance takes place of the battle which ended the Hundred Years' War between France and England. It is one of the largest open-air events of the French summer.

When Aliénor of France married the English king Henry Plantagenet in 1152 – her second marriage – the duchy of Aquitaine was her wedding gift. For more than 300 years, until the battle before the gates of Castillon on 17 July 1453, Aliénor's Aquitaine, the prosperous south-west of France, remained under English rule.

Paradoxically, the inhabitants of Castillon did not themselves take part in this pivotal event in history. Protected behind their city walls, they followed the battle with almost as little involvement as the present-day spectators who watch the pageant.

An open seventeen-acre slope at the foot of the Château de Castegen serves as the stage for this piece of medieval history, just a cannon-shot away from the actual site of the historic battle. The re-enactment of the battle towards the end of the performance makes use of the whole area of the hill, giving the impression more of being on a film set than in a theater.

La bataille – the show

For the two-hour duration of the performance, the spectators immerse themselves in medieval life. They see everyday life on farms and in taverns portrayed with pinpoint accuracy – in the markets, at the grape harvest, and on the hunting parties of the nobility. After the conquest of Bordeaux in 1451 the people of Aquitaine come into conflict with the French soldiers and attempt to defend themselves.

The spectators experience this historic episode from the Abbaye de Saint-Florent, an abbey which by chance stands at the center of the battle which will change the balance of power in Europe.

First of all, the audience feels the concerns of the prior for his flock, then those of the villager worried for his harvest, the nobleman anxious about his lands, and Count Raoul over whether his wife is faithful to him. Finally the battle begins between the English general John Talbot and the troops of Jean Bureau, Charles VII's Master of Artillery.

It is a breathtaking spectacle, lavish with pyrotechnics and other effects. While not all scenes are self-explanatory, this is more than made up for by the magnificent staging of the production as a whole. An audience can, after all, understand an Italian opera without a translation - and children always find the event fascinating.

The website[1] is also available in English, where you can find a short video with clips from the performance.

The drama has been staged on at least a dozen evenings in July and August for over 30 years, and now attracts around 30,000 visitors each season.

That is not to say that it is always the same play; over the years the drama has developed and undergone changes. The most recent

[1]http://www.batailledecastillon.com/index_en.html

has been a gradual transformation between 2008 and 2012, and it now ends with an optimistic outlook on the Renaissance.

'*La Bataille de Castillon*', the association which holds responsibility for the show, goes to enormous lengths on its creation. From the restoration of rare antique objects, to the stage set for the priory, to the production-line creation of shields, swords and pistols, the set-design team works all year long on the production.
More than 800 costumes have been created from records in the Encyclopedia of Eugène Viollet-le-Duc, a French art historian of the 19th century. In addition to these there are aprons, hats, caps and other items of clothing, which all need either repairing or re-placing over the years.

There is another, invisible, side to their efforts: over a number of years, thousands of hours of work have been spent digging up hundreds of yards of the site in order to lay miles of electrical cable and pipes. Castillon-la-Bataille offers both financial and logistical support to the performances.

This is the most successful cultural event in Aquitaine; over the years it has attracted well over 700,000 spectators.

A total of about 700 volunteers from around the region take part, be they the 450 amateur actors and 50 riders on the 'stage', or those working behind the scenes. The scenery is also populated with a good hundred animals: horses, cows, pigs, dogs, goats, donkeys, sheep, doves and geese. Many of them – both human and animal – work the whole year round to ensure the success of the performances. Rehearsals begin in early spring for the actors and riders, as well as any animal training that may still be necessary.

The animals are all trained, just as they would be in a circus. Each animal knows its role, recognizes the music that accompanies its entrance, and becomes downright impatient waiting in the wings.

Alice the sow (a Basque-Bayeux cross) and her companion Chouchou (a Gascon) were chosen some years ago for their rustic, medieval appearance. They have played their roles for so long now that they no longer need any rehearsal. Alice has even developed the habit of announcing her entrance with a series of piercing squeals.

The yoke of Lourdais oxen pulling their cart and the pair of Blonde d'Aquitaines have also long since learned their parts off by heart, and need little help from the trainer. The donkeys, on the other hand, are unpredictable and temperamental fellow actors. The pilgrims hold carrots under their cloaks for them to follow, but they

<u>Dates, Information and Reservations:</u>
Performance dates are usually between mid-July and mid-August.
<u>Admission:</u>
Entry for children under 5 is free, and discounted ticket prices are available for children aged 5-11.
The meal can also be ordered in advance.

Reservations via the 'Bataille' office:
Tel: +33 5 57 40 14 53
Fax: +33 5 57 40 36 48
email: info@batailledecastillon.com

The visit to the performance can be combined with activities in Castillon-la-Bataille in the afternoon. You can visit an exhibition (free of charge) about the Hundred Years War or take part in guided tours of Castillon-la-Bataille and workshops on medieval crafts.

English Guyenne

In 1137, the last duke of Aquitaine dies. His daughter Aliénor becomes the wife of Louis Le Jeune, the future king of France. Shortly after the annulment of this marriage, in 1152, she marries Henry Plantagenet, who becomes King of England. The powerful province is Aliénor's dowry, and thus comes under English rule for the next three centuries. It is a rule characterized by prosperity, which makes Aquitaine richer than ever before.

However, the province remains at the same time a vassal-state of France. Coveted from all sides, Aquitaine is in a constant state of war, being conquered alternately by the English and the French.

In those times, Aquitaine roughly extended over the area covered by the modern regions of Poitou-Charentes, Limousin and Auvergne, as well as the departments of the Vendée, Dordogne and Lot. However, from the 13th century onwards, the Aquitaine of the high medieval period fragmented, leaving Guyenne, which corresponds to modern-day Aquitaine.

During this time, the balance of power in our little Castillon itself constantly went to and fro. For a short period between 1223 and 1259, the town comes under French rule again. From the end of the 13th century, Castillon belongs to the Counts de Foix; Sainte-Foy and Castillon are conquered by Raoul de Nesles. However, in May 1303, in a formal ceremony in the church of Saint-Emilion, the entire province of Guyenne is then returned to the King of England. In 1377, the duke of Anjou, brother to the French king, lays siege to Castillon for two weeks after conquering Bergerac and Sainte-Foy. Castillon is captured, but does not remain long in French hands.

***

Other regions of France also belonged to England at times during this period. Ironically, the Normans were responsible for this, as they had conquered England in the 11th century. As a result, the laws of succession repeatedly brought parts of the continent under the rule of an English king, or caused disputes over the right to the throne.

In the absence of a male heir after the death of Charles IV, Philippe de Valois is declared regent, and then king. The claim of the English king, the son of a French princess, is rejected on the grounds that the Salic law of succession denies women the throne. This is interpreted by the peers of France as a requirement for an unbroken male line (1317, lex salica).

After a number of incidents, Philippe VI occupies Aquitaine in 1337, beginning a war that will last more than a hundred years. The war ravages France and brings it, in financial ruin, to the brink of defeat. Only under the leadership of Joan of Arc does the country reach a turning-point.

In 1450, Normandy reverts to France, leaving Guyenne, as the south-west part of Aquitaine is known, the last part of the country under English rule. Emboldened by Joan of Arc's military successes against the English, Charles VII launches a campaign to conquer the province.

Then in 1451 Jean de Dunois conquers Bordeaux, officially bringing Castillon, along with the whole of Guyenne, under the rule of Charles VII of France. However, Viscount Gaston de Foix of Castillon refuses to submit, and his son, Jean de Foix, joins the league of Bordelais nobility opposed to French rule. They summon the English back, and in 1452 the veteran English general John Talbot arrives with his troops in Bordeaux.

The battle at Castillon on 17 July 1453 marks the final end of the Hundred Years' War – which in reality lasted a decade and a half longer than that – between France and England. Guyenne finally remains a part of France.

The people of the South West could however hardly be said to be happy about this.

Under the English Crown, Aquitaine knew neither poverty nor oppression. The English Magna Carta also applied to them, and entitled them to civil rights way beyond those allowed by the bonds of the French system of estates. The English kings had passed liberal statutes granting the *communes* autonomy; Aquitaine could in no way be regarded as a province occupied by England.

In addition, there was brisk trade with England via the ports of Bordeaux. The export of wine contributed particularly to the prosperity of the region.

Indeed, England was dependent on the wine of Guyenne: England was suffering from climate change, which led to a marked cooling from the 13th century onwards (the Little Ice Age). Suddenly, the cultivation of some crops was impossible – including grapevines, which until that point had thrived all over the south of England. Wine was, however, virtually a staple food, given that in those times it was much safer to drink wine than the hygienically questionable water.

These economic relationships formed the foundation of extremely close ties between England and Bordeaux, in both their mutual interests. It was for this reason that the people of Bordeaux allied themselves with the English in 1451 against the advancing French troops. King Henry VI of England, when he was informed of the sentiments of the people of Aquitaine after the fall of Bordeaux, was also only too glad to commission General Talbot with the task of recapturing the region. The victorious French would later take their revenge: King Charles VII placed a ban on Aquitaine's wine trade with England.

In patriotic France, the play naturally celebrates the outcome of the battle as a success. All the more remarkable, therefore, are the scenes such as the skirmishes between the Castillonais and the French soldiers, openly showing the people of Aquitaine wanting to remain English. Nor are the French portrayed as liberators at the end of the war – rather, they drive the province into poverty.

While the export of wine to England cannot be completely blockaded, it does reduce to a dangerous extent. Voluntary or forced exile thins the ranks of both ordinary citizens and the nobility. The voluntary exiles are, however, welcomed with open arms on their return a few years later. Some even have their surrendered lands returned - including Jean de Foix, the count's son, who had fled to England.

Only in 1461 does the new king of France, Louis XI, restore Aquitaine's ancient rights and privileges and grant it the freedom to trade with England. From 1474 onwards, the Castillonnais gradually have their privileges returned. Jean de Foix-Candale grants them a charter, with the right to elect a mayor and two councils (*ju-rats*). In 1487 this is ratified and extended by Gaston II.

The historic battle

Following Talbot's landing in 1452, Bordeaux and Castillon had opened their gates to the English during the course of a rapid 're-capture' of Guyenne.

In the summer of 1453, the French begin their counter-attack, marching four armies in the direction of Bordeaux. One of them advances through the Dordogne valley, occupying Gensac on 8 July 1453.

This army then approaches a fortified Castillon. The soldiers do not, however, lay siege to it, as was the usual practice through the whole of the Middle Ages and into the early modern period. They no longer wish to conquer Guyenne town by town; they want to annihilate Talbot's army, deciding the fate of Aquitaine in one single operation.

And so the French change their tactics, luring Talbot's army to an area where they have the strategic advantage.

The Bureau brothers know Castillon and the surrounding area well, having attacked the town before in 1451 with Penthièvre's army.

Their army makes camp a little over a mile east of the town, in a valley on the right-hand bank of the Dordogne. It comprises around 10,000 men 'from every province', with 1,800 lances[2] and archers. The artillery, under the command of the Bureau brothers, consists of 300 cannons, operated by 700 soldiers – the numbers alone give an idea of the power the French were able to deploy using these new weapons. The French archers are joined by the thousand-strong Breton army, including a cavalry of 240 lances.

700 Soldiers occupy the Abbey of Saint-Florent in the north-

[2]http://en.wikipedia.org/wiki/Lances_fournies

east of the valley and the Breton cavalry of 240 lances is withdrawn as reinforcements to Horable, a mile to the north.

The position chosen offers unsurpassable advantages. It is backed to the north by the Lidoire, a small stream with steep banks, which can be dammed to raise the water level. To the west, south and east a ditch is dug within the space of three days: a mile long, 16 to 20 feet wide and about 12 feet deep. It is much more than a simple trench; it has recesses to allow crossfire, is protected by an earthwork and reinforced with a palisade, making it a considerable obstacle to the English cavalry. By the time it is finished, the encampment extends 200 to 350 yards from north to south, and around 650 yards from east to west. To the front of the camp an open area extends for 550 to 650 yards until it reaches the Dordogne River, which can only be crossed at one point: a ford called the *pas de Rauzan*.

Should the enemy approach from the north, he will come to a halt at the Lidoire; crossing will be difficult and put him in close proximity to the encampment. Should he come from the west, he will be unable to spread out fully against the narrow frontage, only 200 yards wide. Approaching from the south, the battlefield lies un-protected, under the fire of the French cannons all the way to the Dordogne River.

This is the encampment that Talbot is to attack; it is essentially an artillery park.

The English army is of comparable size, if not superior; Talbot can muster at least 6,000 men in Bordeaux, as well as a further 3,000 Gascons who join his troops shortly before the attack.

But Talbot makes the mistake of sending his troops to attack the French camp at intervals as they arrive at the battlefield. In the end he has 4,000 soldiers in place: still too few to take the enemy's well-prepared position in one fell swoop.

While still in Bordeaux, Talbot had been informed by the Castillonais of the arrival of the French army and had decided to relieve the town.

He spends the night at Libourne, and on the morning of 17 July he reaches the woods above the priory. Doing as the Castillonais had advised him, he storms the vulnerable garrison at Saint-Florent. Its occupants flee, retreating to the encampment on the Lidoire. The English pursue them along the mountain flank above the stream, but after bloody hand-to-hand combat the retreating soldiers cross the small river and are immediately inside the encampment.

Surprised, perhaps, by the difficulties they encounter, the English retreat for the time being to the priory. They gather supplies, and break open some of the wine barrels abandoned by the French.

Talbot is just about to hear mass when he receives the news that the French are leaving the camp. Indeed, unmistakable clouds of dust are rising in the east, above the position held by the French. They will only discover later that this was the pages moving the baggage train out of the way of the battle. Believing his enemy to be on the move, Talbot does not hesitate any longer. He advances the troops currently available to him, intending to put the French to flight.

Pushing forward to the embankment, the English attempt to raise Talbot's banner at the entrance to the French camp, but in the close fighting it falls into the ditch.

Under the command of brothers Gaspard and Jean Bureau (the latter is King Charles VII's commander-in-chief of artillery), the French artillery has had time to prepare. Three hundred cannons fire simultaneously; they are loaded with '*mitrailles*' – cylinders filled with lead pellets, much like enormous shot cartridges.

The carnage is appalling. The attackers are standing so close together that they can neither escape the cannon-fire nor scatter. The survivors re-form ranks, but the French cannons are soon reloaded.

Talbot's own artillery is too slow to reach the battlefield in time. Under fire from the French, the English and Gascon troops fight for a further hour. Feeling summoned to battle by the thunder of the cannon, the Breton cavalry, waiting in Horable as reinforcements, now attack. They fall upon the fleeing English and massacre them.

The French then open the barricades and pursue the English. In the melée, Talbot's horse is shot. As he falls, he is hit by a French archer, and finally killed by a blow to the head with an axe. Talbot's son, Lord L'Isle, also falls.

There are at least 4,000 dead left on the battlefield. The survivors flee; some try to cross the Dordogne river, where many drown. Others break off to the west, some reaching Saint-Émilion. A further number go into hiding within the fortifications at Castillon. This proves to be a short-lived refuge; on 18 July the French advance on Castillon with their artillery, and the town surrenders.

Once news of Talbot's death spreads, all the towns still held by the English concede defeat, and Bordeaux gives up without a fight. The English capitulation is signed in the castle of Pressac, in Saint-Étienne-de-Lisse.

Not only is the war at an end; the kings of England will never again take possession in France.

The end of knightly warfare

The play also portrays the myth that the English soldiers were not entirely fit for battle because they had emptied the wine cellar at the Abbaye de Saint Florent on the evening before the battle.

In reality, the defeat of the English was brought about by the new style of warfare waged by the French – in particular, the massive deployment of artillery in open pitched battle. The late medieval period was one of rapidly developing technological progress, including both weapons technology and warfare.

Up until this point, warfare in Europe had fundamentally consisted of two elements:

The conquest of fortified cities by siege. Here the besieged were as a rule well advised to surrender, as this allowed them to negotiate somewhat tolerable terms.

In contrast, the Bureau brothers' strategy in Guyenne makes protracted and laborious town-by-town conquest unnecessary. If the enemy forces are defeated and no longer able to defend them, the towns' resistance is useless.

The second element was the battles between armies of knights. From a modern perspective, these were astonishingly unbloody, as their aim was not in any way to destroy the opponent. Quite the opposite: each knight did his best to keep his enemy alive. There was a completely banal reason for this: a ransom could be negotiated for a prisoner. This was how knights maintained their livelihood.

This was the simple foundation of the concept of 'knightly' warfare.

This comes to an end at the battle of Crécy in August 1346, when the English do not meet the French soldiers in knightly single combat. Instead, they send their archers to the front, who decimate the advancing knights with their arrows. At this point in history the English longbow is mechanically superior to the French bow, and has a significantly greater range.

After the battle, the French complain of the dishonorable behavior of the English.

Up until this point, the French had been the most numerous and the most warlike knights of all Europe, and they had joined this battle with the intention, once again, of taking their noble opponents prisoner and filling their coffers with ransom money.

Now, of course, they cannot turn the clock back; they must themselves adapt to the new way of fighting.

Charles VII uses the truce negotiated in Tours in 1444 to reorganize his army. Back in 1438, the Estates General had already granted the king the power to raise money without requiring their consent each year, as had previously been the case. This began in the regions of the *langue d'Oil* in the north in 1438 and 1443, then in the *langue d'Oc* in 1439. This gave him a kind of General Power – and introduced permanent taxation. From then on, the king had the means to maintain a standing army. Above all, he could avoid having demobilized mercenaries marauding through his country.

From 1445 onwards, he has the army organized into basic units – 'lances' – which operate as a team using several different weapons. They consist of a knight, accompanied by two mounted archers, a man armed with a sword and a long dagger, together with a non-combatant page and a servant. One hundred lances form a company. His standing army starts as 15 companies – 9,000 men. They are stationed in garrisons which the towns must support, so that the royal coffers are not burdened in peacetime.

It was always the civilian population that had to bear the burdens of war. The countryside through which an army moved was routinely plundered – a simple necessity, in order to feed and finance themselves. It was a matter of total indifference to them whether it was their own country or the enemy's. A vivid depiction of the way this used to happen can be found in Jean Anouil's *'Conjuration des Importants'*, in the chapter in which his hero follows the French army on the way to Rocroy.

From 1448 onwards, every parish of 50 households is required to provide and equip a trained archer. In return, this man is exempt from taxes, hence the term *'franc-archer'*. In the end, the king has around 8,000 men at his disposal, and an army of archers which can match that of the English. As in the past, he has additional mercenaries hired when he needs them. Besides these, he also has a standing Scottish guard. In total, Charles VII has 15,000 mobile, well-trained cavalrymen. With every battle that passes, there are also fewer English archers left standing, especially as their training requires considerable time.

Jean Bureau, Charles VII's commander-in-chief of artillery, had been reorganizing France's field artillery since 1439 to promote the deployment of cannons. Artillery had previously been used primarily during sieges.

More recent advances in technology had, however, led to the development of cannons that were relatively easy to transport. In addition to their new mobility, a distinguishing feature of these weapons was a greater impact depth, against which the knights' armor was ultimately useless.

Jean Bureau and his brother personally command both the artillery and the archers in every battle in Normandy and Guyenne. In Castillon, for the first time in the western world, Jean Bureau deploys the cannons on a massive scale in open pitched battle.

The battle before the gates of Castillon thus ultimately marks the end of the way the European world had waged war up until that point. The artillery is superior to the medieval concept of warfare. Hand-to-hand single combat becomes less important, and the knights' suits of armor become useless.

Attractions near Castillon-la-Bataille

If you have time to spare, it is worth spending an extra day or two in the area.

Castillon, renamed Castillon-la-Bataille in 1953, sits on a strategically important crossing over the Dordogne near Libourne, on the border between the Bordelais and the Périgord. Today it is a small town with close to 3,000 inhabitants.

The baroque church and the 12th-century chapel of Sainte Marguerite in Capitourlan are worth seeing.

Town website: http://www.castillonlabataille.fr/

Information, including details of current tours and events, can be found at the Tourist office

https://www.tourisme-castillonpujols.fr/

***

Castillon-la-Bataille gives its name to the wine appellation **Castillon Côtes de Bordeaux**, which is cultivated in nine *communes* over an area of 7,040 acres. This appellation was separated from the Bordeaux appellation in 1989.

In 1060, one of the viscounts of Guyenne had invited a number of Benedictine monks from Saint Florent de Saumur to Castillon. They built their monastery to the north of the castle, also naming it Saint Florent, and became well known for their wine.

More information about the wines can be found on the appellation's website:

http://castillon-cotesdebordeaux.com/index.htm

There is a *Maison du Vin* in Castillon-la-Bataille. It is open Monday to Friday from 9am to 6pm.

Maison des vins des côtes de Castillon
6 allées de la République 33350 Castillon La Bataille
Tel: +33 5 57 40 00 88
Fax: +33 5 57 40 06 31
e-mail: contact@castillon-cotesdebordeaux.com

***

Less than 6 miles away is the castle of **Michel de Montaigne** (1533-1592), one of the greatest minds of the French Renaissance. The château was devastated by a fire in 1885. It has been partially restored, but only the tower is open to visitors. It houses an exhibition about Montaigne, including the room in which he died. It is open daily from 10am to 6:30pm from 1st July to 24th August, and from Wednesday to Sunday at most other times in the year. Guided tours of the tower last around 45 minutes.

Château de Montaigne
24230 Saint-Michel-de-Montaigne
Contact: 05 53 58 63 93 info@chateau-montaigne.com
The website is also available in English.

http://www.chateau-montaigne.com/

***

Just 8 miles away is **Saint-Émilion**, center for one of the premium *appellation d'origine protégée* wines of the Haut-Médoc. Founded in the 8th century by a monk named Émilion, the town was a center of religious life.

Today the town is a UNESCO World Heritage Site, and it has an impressive array of countless monuments and buildings, predominantly from the Romanesque period. On first impression, this town with its monuments and artefacts from the Romanesque period appears to be an open-air museum. There is, however, a second 'museum' – a vast underground labyrinth.

Alongside extensive catacombs in the underground St Émilion – *St Émilion souterrain* – the largest underground church in Europe is also open daily to visitors. The visit lasts just under an hour. Above ground, a 1½-hour guided tour of the historic town center is available every day except Sunday. Both tours are only available in French, but there is a shorter version of the two in English, lasting 1½ hours in total.

There are also a number of thematic events such as "Une nuit sous la révolution", a nocturnal tour that leads to underground hiding places of the insurgents during the Great Revolution.

A visit to the underground Saint-Émilion is also included in a day-long wine tour which takes place every Saturday from the beginning of April to the beginning of November. For this reason, these 'Oenology Saturdays' are subtitled 'The best of Saint-Émilion in one day'. In addition to the catacombs, the day comprises an introduction to viticulture in the wine school, a meal with winetasting and a visit to a vineyard. This program is not available to under-age children.

The wine school can be visited independently of the day-tour – open daily from mid-July to the end of August.

Ticket reservations, accommodation and further information are available from the town's website:

http://www.saint-emilion-tourisme.com/

Further Reading

Click here for a longer Bibliography with sources 'Sur l'histoire de la Guyenne' and 'Sur la période de la guerre de Cent Ans et de la Guyenne anglaise': http://benito.p.free.fr/biblio.html

Revue Historique de Bordeaux: Available via open Edition: http://search.openedition.org/index.php?op[]=AND&q[]=+Revue+Historique+de+Bordeaux&field[]=All

The Hundred Years' War on Wikipedia
_https://en.wikipedia.org/wiki/Hundred_Years%27_War

The history of Aquitaine on Wikipedia
https://fr.wikipedia.org/wiki/Aquitaine (French) or (a shorter version in English)
https://en.wikipedia.org/wiki/Aquitaine

About the author

Annemarie Nikolaus is a social scientist. Among other things, she has studied history and journalism. After a long career as a journalist, she began writing literature at the start of 2001. Since 2011 most of her works have been published independently.

Born in Hesse, Germany, she lived for twenty years in northern Italy before moving to the Auvergne in France with her daughter in 2010.

Interested in up-to-date information on her books and new publications? Subscribe to her Newsletter:
http://eepurl.com/bHQtvf

You can find Annemarie on the internet here:
Blog in English: http://bit.ly/2G0ugGJ
Patreon: www.patreon.com/AnnemarieNikolaus
Facebook: www.facebook.com/AnnemarieNikolaus.Autorin
Twitter: http://twitter.com/AnneNikolaus

****

Publications:

In English:

Magical Stories. Short stories for children. Paperback edition ISBN 9782902412600.

Radiant Hope. Illustrated science-fiction story. Paperback edition ISBN 9782902412600.

The Granddaughter. *"Quick, quick, slow - Lietzensee Dance Club"*. Paperback edition ISBN 9782493398123

Back onto the Dance Floor. *"Quick, quick, slow - Lietzensee Dance Club"*. Paperback edition ISBN 9782493398147.

Falling for a movie star. *"Quick, quick, slow - Lietzensee Dance Club"*. Paperback edition ISBN 9782493398130

Broken Rules. Historical crime short stories. Paperback edition ISBN 9782902412686

Silenced. Short thriller. Paperback edition ISBN 978-xx

Gone... Short Stories. Paperback edition ISBN 9782902412877.

The Piratess. *"Dragon World"* series. Fantasy novel. Paperback edition ISBN 9782902412679

Aquitaine: The End of a War. *"By The Wayside..."* series. Paperback edition ISBN 9782902412808

In German:

Novels and short stories

Historical

Königliche Republik. Historical novel. Paperback edition ISBN 9782902412471

Verjährt. Historical crime short stories. Paperback edition ISBN 9782902412549.

Fantasy

Die Piratin. „*Drachenwelt*" series. Fantasy novel. Paperback edition ISBN 9782902412495

Das Feuerpferd. Fantasy novel, together with Monique Lhoir und Sabine Abel. Paperback edition ISBN 9782902412501

Magische Geschichten. Short stories for children and adults. Paperback edition ISBN 9782902412488

Renntag in Kruschar. „*Drachenwelt*" series. Fantasy anthology. E-Book only

Leuchtende Hoffnung. A Science Fiction novel in Advent calendar form. Paperback edition ISBN 9782902412563

Mystery

Ustica. Short story thriller. Paperback edition ISBN 9782902412556.

Bitterer Wein. »Médoc« series. Mystery. Paperback edition ISBN 782493398017

Haus zu verkaufen. Family drama. Paperback edition ISBN 9782902412983

Tot. Short stories. Paperback edition ISBN 9782902412587.

Verjährt. (see above)

Romance

Die Enkelin. '*Quick, quick, slow - Tanzclub Lietzensee*' series. Love story. Paperback edition ISBN 9782493398093.

Flirt mit einem Star. '*Quick, quick, slow - Tanzclub Lietzensee*' series. Love story. Paperback edition ISBN 9782493398109

Zurück aufs Parkett. '*Quick, quick, slow - Tanzclub Lietzensee*' series. Story of love and marriage. Paperback edition ISBN 9782493398116

Non-fiction

Tourist attractions

Aquitanien: Das Ende eines Krieges. '*Am Rande des Weges ...*' series. Paperback edition ISBN 9782902412570

Background series on literature and books

Suche Reisebegleitung. *Fliegende Blätter.* Paperback edition ISBN 9781499608427

Junge Welten. *Fliegende Blätter.* Paperback edition ISBN 9781500971991

For publications in other languages please check the shops

35

Photo credits:

My thanks go to '*La Bataille de Castillon*' for the event photos. Copyright: 2010 Jean-Bernard Nadeau

Cover: Photo Copyright 2010 Jean-Bernard Nadeau.

Coat of Arms: Copyright Peter17 [GFDL (http://www.gnu.org/copyleft/fdl.html), CC-BY-SA-3.0 (http://creativecommons.org/licenses/by-sa/3.0/) or CC-BY-2.5 (http://creativecommons.org/licenses/by/2.5)], via Wikimedia Commons

Château de Montaigne: Copyright Henry SALOMÉ [GFDL (http://www.gnu.org/copyleft/fdl.html) or CC-BY-SA-3.0-2.5-2.0-1.0 (http://creativecommons.org/licenses/by-sa/3.0)], via Wikimedia Commons

www.ingramcontent.com/pod-product-compliance
Lightning Source LLC
LaVergne TN
LVHW010911200726
843507LV00002B/580